PELICAN BOOKS

A 250

CONTEMPORARY BRITISH ART

HERBERT READ

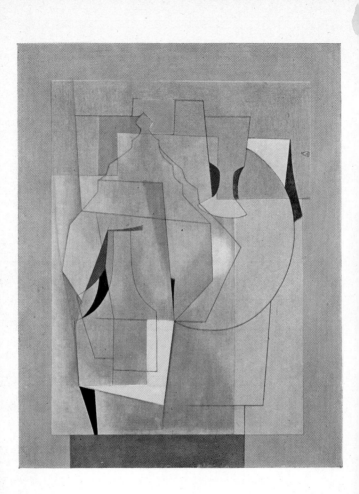

1. BEN NICHOLSON: Still-life (Dolomites). 1950

Contemporary
British Art

*

HERBERT READ

PENGUIN BOOKS

FIRST PUBLISHED IN 1951

Made and Printed in Great Britain
for Penguin Books Ltd
Harmondsworth · Middlesex
by Hunt, Barnard and Co Ltd

CONTENTS

LIST OF PLATES

In Colour

1 BEN NICHOLSON
 STILL-LIFE (DOLOMITES). 1950. Oil. 48 by 38 in.
 Collection: The Artist

2 WILLIAM SCOTT
 STILL-LIFE WITH COLLANDER AND BEANS.
 1948. Oil. 32 by 26 in. *Collection: Howard Bliss, Esq.*

3 IVON HITCHENS
 RECLINING NUDE. 1947. Oil. $23\frac{1}{2}$ by $28\frac{1}{2}$ in.
 Collection: James Escott, Esq.

4 DAVID JONES
 THE GENTLE BIRD. 1950. Water-colour. 31 by
 27 in. *Collection: The Contemporary Art Society*

5 ROBERT MACBRYDE
 TABLE IN A RED ROOM. 1950. Oil. 30 by 24 in.
 Collection: The Arts Council of Great Britain

6 GRAHAM SUTHERLAND
 STANDING FORM. 1950. Oil. $52\frac{1}{2}$ by 46 in. *Collection: The Artist*

In Black and White

1 AUGUSTUS JOHN, O.M.
 PORTRAIT OF MATTHEW SMITH. 1947–8. Oil.
 24 by 20 in. *Collection: The Tate Gallery*

2 JACOB EPSTEIN
   VAUGHAN WILLIAMS, O.M. 1950. Bronze.
   Height: 15½ in. *Collection: The Arts Council of Great
   Britain*

3 KARIN JONZEN
   BUST. 1949. Terracotta. Height: 18 in. *Collection:
   East Riding Education Committee*

4 LAWRENCE GOWING
   MISS BAKER. 1948. Oil. 29½ by 21½ in. *Collection:
   The Arts Council of Great Britain*

5 WILLIAM COLDSTREAM
   PORTRAIT OF MRS G. A. AUDEN. 1937. Oil.
   30 by 20 in. *Collection: The Contemporary Art Society*

6 RODRIGO MOYNIHAN
   STILL-LIFE WITH FIGURE. 1943. Oil. 39½ by
   32 in. *Collection: The British Council*

7 MATTHEW SMITH
   ELIZABETH RAYNHAM. 1941. Oil. 24 by 19¼ in.
   Collection: Major E. O. Kay

8 LUCIAN FREUD
   GIRL WITH ROSES. 1947–8. Oil. 41½ by 29½ in.
   Collection: The British Council

9 RUSKIN SPEAR, A.R.A.
   BARMAID. 1947. Oil. 19 by 11 in. *Collection: Mrs
   John Stenson*

10 CLAUDE ROGERS
   NUDE. 1937. Oil. 19½ by 23 in. *Collection: The
   Contemporary Art Society*

11 CERI RICHARDS
THE RED SKIRT. 1949. Oil. $36\frac{1}{2}$ by $53\frac{1}{2}$ in. *Collection: The Arts Council of Great Britain*

12 H. E. DU PLESSIS
RUSSELL SQUARE. 1945. Oil. $19\frac{1}{2}$ by $23\frac{1}{4}$ in. *Collection: Mrs Du Plessis*

13 EDWARD BAWDEN
A DRY MOAT. 1948. Pen, ink and water-colour. 18 by 22 in. *Collection: The British Council*

14 JOHN NASH, A.R.A.
THE RIVER BRETT, HIGHAM. 1950. Oil. 27 by 34 in. *Collection: W. S. Cowell Ltd*

15 W. G. GILLIES
GRUINARD. 1948. Water-colour. 29 by 35 in. *Collection: Dr R. Willie*

16 L. S. LOWRY
INDUSTRIAL CITY. 1948. Oil. 24 by 30 in. *Collection: The British Council*

17 VIVIAN PITCHFORTH
NIGHT TRANSPORT. 1940. Oil. 20 by $29\frac{7}{8}$ in. *Collection: The Chantrey Bequest*

18 WILLIAM TOWNSEND
SOUTH BANK. 1948. Oil. 25 by 30 in. *Collection: The Artist*

19 TRISTRAM HILLIER
FISHING BOATS. 1946. Oil. 24 by 32 in. *Collection: The Bradford City Art Gallery*

20 KENNETH ROWNTREE

LION DINING-ROOMS. 1949. Water-colour. $14\frac{1}{2}$ by $18\frac{1}{4}$ in. *Collection: Festival of Britain, 1951*

21 BATESON MASON

FULHAM BY MOONLIGHT. 1949. Oil. $17\frac{1}{2}$ by $27\frac{1}{2}$ in. *Collection: The Leicester Galleries*

22 JOHN MINTON

LONDON BRIDGE. *c.* 1945. Brush and pen drawing – Indian ink with touches of body colour. **19** by $24\frac{3}{4}$ in. *Collection: The British Council*

23 LEONARD APPLEBEE

BETHANIA. 1947. Oil. 30 by 40 in. *Collection: The British Council*

24 MARY POTTER

JESSAMINE. 1943. Oil. 24 by 30 in. *Collection: The National Gallery of New South Wales*

25 WINIFRED NICHOLSON

HONEYSUCKLE AND SWEET PEAS – Contrast of Pinks. *c.* 1930. Oil. $17\frac{1}{2}$ by 28 in. *Collection: The Aberdeen Art Gallery*

26 JOHN PIPER

CHELTENHAM: COMPOSITE OF HOUSES IN PRIORY PARADE. MURAL FOR THE BRITISH EMBASSY, RIO DE JANEIRO, BRAZIL. 1950. Oil. 6 ft. 7 in. by 4 ft. 9 in. *Collection: The Ministry of Works*

27 ALAN DAVIE

MUSIC OF THE AUTUMN LANDSCAPE. 1948. Oil. $49\frac{1}{4}$ by $37\frac{1}{2}$ in. *Collection: Miss Peggy Guggenheim*

2. WILLIAM SCOTT:
Still-life with Collander
and Beans. 1948

28 ROBERT MEDLEY
A SUMMER DAY. 1950. Oil. 52½ by 62½ in. *Collection: The Hanover Gallery*

29 JOHN WELLS
OLD SEA PORT. 1949. Oil and pencil. 15¾ by 17¾ in. *Collection: The Artist*

30 PATRICK HERON
THE ROUND TABLE. 1950. Oil. 35½ by 17½ in. *Collection: The Arts Council of Great Britain*

31 PRUNELLA CLOUGH
FISHERMEN IN A BOAT. 1949. Oil. 55 by 30 in. *Collection: Dr H. M. Roland*

32 JOHN ARMSTRONG
ENCOUNTER. 1947. Tempera. 20 by 24 in. *Collection: The Artist*

33 BRYAN WYNTER
FORESHORE WITH GULLS. 1949. Water-colour. 11½ by 17¾ in. *Collection: The British Council*

34 JOHN TUNNARD
WEATHER FORECAST. 1945. Oil. 23 by 21½ in. *Collection: Sir David Scott*, K.C.M.G.

35 PETER LANYON
PORTREATH. 1949. Oil. 30 by 30 in. *Collection: Miss Phyllis Bottome*

36 EDWARD BURRA
ST PETER AND THE HIGH PRIEST'S SERVANT. 1950. Water-colour. 52½ by 40½ in. *Collection: The Lefevre Gallery*

37 ROY DE MAISTRE
THE DEPOSITION. 1946. Oil. 56 by 44¼ in. *Collection: The British Council*

38 WYNDHAM LEWIS
THE ARMADA. 1937. Oil. 36 by 28 in. *Collection: The Lefevre Gallery*

39 WILLIAM ROBERTS
THE MOTHERS. 1944. Water-colour. 20 by 14 in. *Collection: The Leicester Galleries*

40 EDWARD LE BAS, A.R.A.
BARMAID AT THE GARRICK. 1944. Oil. 20 by 24 in. *Collection: The Artist*

41 GEOFFREY TIBBLE
PAY DAY. 1950. Oil. 20 by 24 in. *Collection: Arthur Tooth & Sons Ltd*

42 STANLEY SPENCER
THE ANGELS OF THE APOCALYPSE. 1949. Oil. 24 by 35 in. *Collection: Mr and Mrs Tully Grigg*

43 MICHAEL AYRTON
AFTERNOON IN ISCHIA. 1947. Oil. 32 by 53½ in. *Collection: The British Council*

44 F. E. McWILLIAM
FATHER AND DAUGHTER. 1949. Concrete. Height: 3 ft. 7 in. *Collection: Mr and Mrs R. J. Sainsbury*

45 FRANK DOBSON, A.R.A.
STUDY FOR LEISURE. 1950. Terracotta. Height: 12 ft. *Collection: The Artist*

46 JOHN CRAXTON
GALATAS. 1947. Oil. 30 by 40 in. *Collection: The British Council*

47 KEITH VAUGHAN
OYSTER FISHERMAN, NO. 1. 1947–8. Gouache-Indian ink. 14½ by 19½ in. *Collection: The British Council*

48 ROBERT COLQUHOUN
GIRL WITH A CIRCUS GOAT. 1948. Oil. 30 by 25 in. *Collection: The British Council*

49 LOUIS LE BROCQUY
MAN CREATING A BIRD. 1948. Oil. 24 by 20 in. *Collection: James Bomford, Esq*

50 MICHAEL ROTHENSTEIN
COCKEREL AND PLOUGH. 1950. Water-colour. 15 by 23 in. *Collection: The Artist*

51 MERLYN EVANS
THE JAIL. 1950. Oil. 24 by 36 in. *Collection: The Felton Bequest*

52 W. BARNS-GRAHAM
UPPER GLACIER. 1950. Oil. 15½ by 24¾ in. *Collection: The British Council*

53 S. W. HAYTER
SEA MYTH. 1946–7. Etching. 11 by 15½ in. *Collection: Bibliotheque Nationale, Paris, and Museum of Modern Art, New York*

54 WILLIAM GEAR
BLACK TREE. 1950. Oil. 39½ by 32 in. *Collection: Gimpel Fils Gallery, London*

CONTEMPORARY BRITISH ART

AS it is difficult to indicate in a title the intention of a small book like this, the reader will perhaps allow me an explanatory paragraph. My general purpose is to give a report on the situation of the arts of painting and sculpture in Great Britain at the mid-point of the Twentieth Century. This sounds rather portentous, but though the reader will not expect the impersonal objectivity appropriate to an official report, I use formal phraseology to describe my aim because this is not a record of my personal opinions. It is an attempt to write history without the advantage of historical perspective. It is more than likely that when another half century has gone, the situation of British art in 1951 will look astonishingly different. Art criticism, as one may realize by comparing the art criticism of Diderot or Baudelaire with their literary criticism, has its peculiar frailty, and for that reason I try to avoid dogmatic judgements on individual artists, and seek rather to trace significant movements and groupings. Of course, by including a particular painter or sculptor in this or that group, or leaving him out of all groups, I am expressing a preference of a kind; but short of omitting all names, I know of no way of escaping this danger. But the inclusion or exclusion of particular names, or the illustration of the work of particular artists, must not be taken as an act of aesthetic judgement on my part, or as in any sense 'the making of a grade'. I am well aware of the responsibility one assumes in this matter, especially in a medium so widely diffused as a Pelican book. But there are definite limitations of space, and into that space must go, not works of art arranged in an order of merit, but illustrations that throw significant light on the historical situation with which we are dealing. In this way I may well exclude Mr X, whose work in a traditional style I admire, and include Mr Y for whose experimental style I feel no immediate sympathy.

The modern period in British art may be said to date from the year 1910, when the first Post-Impressionist Exhibition was held in London. At that time Post-Impressionism had no established followers in our country. The first decade of the century had been dominated by two Celtic romanticists, Frank Brangwyn and Augustus John, and by a Jewish sculptor, Jacob Epstein. The two painters may to some extent have been influenced by Gauguin; of John it was possible to say, thirty years ago, that 'he is, so to speak, a Post-Impressionist without knowing it'.* Epstein is essentially an Expressionist in a sense I propose to define. But apart from these three eminent individualists, the artists of that decade were engaged in what Charles Marriott, in another happy phrase, has called 'the domestication of French Impressionism without prejudice to the native tradition'. This was the activity on which were engaged such considerable artists as Wilson Steer (one of the founders, in 1885, of the New English Art Club), Walter Sickert, and a group, already breaking away from Impressionism, calling themselves the Neo-Realists. This term was used to characterize the work of the Camden Town Group (Harold Gilman, Robert Bevan, Spencer Gore and Charles Ginner), as well as Sickert and his pupils (sometimes referred to as the Fitzroy Street Group).

In March 1914, the first exhibition of a newly constituted London Group, embracing all these artists, was held at the Goupil Gallery. Though the new group was dominated by the neo-realists (Gilman was the first president, Bevan the treasurer), nevertheless there was no doubt about its general tendency. Post-Impressionism was now a coherent movement in England. It is worth recording that among the members of the hanging committee of this first exhibition of the London Group were Jacob Epstein and Wyndham Lewis.

*Charles Marriott, in *Modern Movements in Painting*, London, 1920.

The London Group still exists, and though it has given birth to other groups (Group X, for example) which generally expressed a determination to keep pace with developments in Paris, their neo-realism has remained one of the dominant tendencies of the past forty years. But movements in art always begin with a bang and end in a whimper, and where to-day shall we look for the disciples of Gilman and Sickert? Conservative critics (not to be confused with academic critics, who are not so perceptive) usually regard Sickert as the greatest painter we have produced in England since Turner. Radical critics like Roger Fry and Clive Bell, while full of appreciation for a painter who could so successfully transplant the art of Degas, and whose genius was always harmoniously evident, nevertheless had to point out that the rejection of Cézanne by Sickert and his friends was a decisive act of suicide. The image is too violent, for what they nevertheless created still remains. That is to say, their values remain, the values of a period; but after the First World War these ceased to have any considerable influence on the development of painting in Great Britain.*

What should now be emphasized is the fact that the whole of this generation derived its inspiration from the French School. It is true that the French School, a generation earlier, had taken deep draughts of inspiration from England – from Constable, Bonington and Turner. But it seemed as though English art had to be transplanted to another soil before it could revive. It had absorbed Impressionism and then, without returning to native sources, it fell under the influence of Cézanne, and of the Post-Impressionists generally – of Fauvism, Cubism, Futurism; of Matisse, Picasso, Braque and Derain. The years after the

*There was, it is true, an attempt to re-establish these values during the brief existence of the Euston Road School (1937–9). This group of master-painters was founded by Graham Bell, William Coldstream, Victor Pasmore and Claude Rogers, and was a conscious protest against the tyrannical influence of the 'School of Paris'. But though these artists felt that 'an unprejudiced approach to the objective world' was still possible, the means they adopted (the exploitation of certain mannerisms of Degas) did not prove to be very convincing. One of the founders, Victor Pasmore, has since become an exponent of abstract art.

war of 1914–18 saw the rise of a school of English painting which, whatever provincial, national or personal accents it might display, remained in its essential style a derivative from the School of Paris.

An exception should perhaps be made of Wyndham Lewis. Lewis had spent some years in Paris, and he had returned, about 1912, with a geometrical style of his own to which he gave the name *Vorticism*. The Vorticist movement which he founded was short-lived, and unfortunately it remained largely a one-man show – Edward Wadsworth, Lewis's ablest supporter in the plastic arts, was essentially dilettante, and his cubism was soon to degenerate into a banal decorative art; and Frederick Etchells, one of the most intelligent members of the group, became an ecclesiastical architect. But while Vorticism lasted it was a vitalizing influence, perhaps the most lively effort ever made to infuse our timid English aestheticism with Latin intellectualism. It failed because there was some disparity of sense and sensibility. Like the Italian Futurists, the English Vorticists tried to take the mind by assault, forgetting that art wins its positions by subtle infiltration. In 1920 that kind of strategy seemed more necessary than, shall we say, the relatively polite *fauvism* of a Matthew Smith. The original 'Fauves' (Braque, Derain, Dufy, Friesz, Marquet, Matisse, Vlaminck) were, as the name implies, considered 'wild'; but their wildness was in their brush-strokes rather than in their minds. They had no ideology to correspond with the manifestos on politics, war, and everything else that were issued by the Futurists and our unique Vorticist. A painter like Matthew Smith is primarily interested in – paint. His sympathies were so much with the Fauvists that for the best part of his life he has preferred to live in the same Mediterranean environment. His affinities are with Matisse and Derain; the female nude and the Provençal landscape are his favourite subjects. There is an element of plastic violence, of rich saturation in reds and blacks, which make his technique superficially similar to the technique of the

3. IVON HITCHENS:
Reclining Nude. 1947

Expressionists; but though this might be attributed to the artist's Nordic sensibility (Matthew Smith is a Yorkshireman), it is no doubt unconscious.

Not so simple, because remaining essentially feminine, and having a peasant or folk-art quality which is universal rather than specifically English or French, is the case of Frances Hodgkins, who late in life – she was born in New Zealand in 1870 and died in 1947 – developed one of the richest styles in English painting, but again a style which owes a good deal to the School of Paris, where she lived for a number of years.

More indigenous, in spite of his affinities with a Vorticist like Lewis, is William Roberts. Born in 1895, the son of a London carpenter, he won a scholarship for drawing, and proceeded to the Slade School of Art. He there discovered the Post-Impressionists and quite early in his career adopted a style and a content to which he has remained faithful all these years. The content is the social life of London – the Cockney in his daily round of work and play; but the style is that aspect of Cubism which we associate most particularly with the work of Fernand Léger; a somewhat mechanized, tubular distortion of the human figure, which yet, in Roberts's case, retains a good deal of humorous characterization. Roberts is often charged with a lack of imaginative development; one might equally praise him for a firmness and consistency lacking in most modern artists. But there he is – a very typical representative of the decisive influence of French post-impressionism on modern English art.

Finally in this group, but as a much more ambiguous figure, I would place Paul Nash, who died in 1946. The work of a painter like Paul Nash might be studied as a duel between his native inclinations, which place him in the quiet tradition of the English water-colourists of the eighteenth and early nineteenth century, and his continual awareness of the excitements of Paris. Sometimes the two influences combine with happy effect, but in general his

C*

strength lies in those landscapes, often conscious of more than the eye sees, which are executed in the characteristic technique of the English water-colourists. Nash had a perfect mastery of this medium, and most of his work follows in the tradition of English water-colourists like Girtin and Cotman. Even when he painted in oils, his pale tonality and clear articulation of colour-values were reminiscent of the technique of the English water-colourists. I do not wish to imply that Paul Nash was merely a traditionalist: his work has a poetic content which is quite original, and in both wars he showed himself capable of wresting beauty from the very heart of horror and tragedy. His most characteristic work, however, is best described as poetic, and a certain love of irrational phantasy enabled Nash to associate himself at one time with the surrealist movement.

There are many more painters who might be placed in the group that derives its inspiration from the School of Paris, and some of them, like Vanessa Bell and Duncan Grant, would normally be treated at some length in any comprehensive account of modern English painting. But I am bound to keep to broad outlines, and I have perhaps given sufficient guide-posts to indicate *one* very considerable range of artistic activity in England. For the past fifty years or more this orientation of art towards Paris – towards the Mediterranean we might even say – has been predominant. I believe that a change of orientation is now taking place, but before I can indicate its nature, I must be allowed to indulge in a few generalizations.

In northern Europe, particularly in Scandinavia and Germany, the modern movement in art has been associated with the word *Expressionism*. Expressionism is not, like impressionism or post-impressionism, a specifically modern style in art. It is rather a style that tends to reappear in the north whenever the strength of external influences diminishes; and unless an artist of the north is very exotic, there is generally a strain of expressionism discernible in his work. But the renaissance of expressionism which we

ociate with the names of a Norwegian, Edward Munch,
a Dutchman, Vincent van Gogh, did not reach Eng-
; our most northern artists, the Scots, have as a matter
ct been the most slavish followers of French impres-
ism or French fauvism (W. McTaggart, S. J. Peploe,
. Ferguson). The somewhat anomalous position of an
t like Stanley Spencer is explained by the expression-
c quality of his work, which has never been recognized
uch, certainly not by himself. Stanley Spencer is perhaps
y to be explained as an English eccentric. He can be re-
ted to other English eccentrics – William Blake and
olman Hunt – and he has the defects, as well as the virtues,
of his type. In the technical sense the plastic arts gain from
the widest basis of experiment and comparison, and for a
painter to ignore the discoveries of a Cézanne or a Picasso
is equivalent to a scientist ignoring the discoveries of an
Einstein or a Freud. But what is gained from seclusion, from
intensive contemplation, and from obstinate independence
is, objectively, an intensity of vision and, subjectively, a
visionary intensity. The English landscape (not its hills and
wooded plains, but the cottage garden and village green) is
recorded with a loving precision; and brooding in this still-
ness the painter conjures up images to illustrate the
universal themes of death and resurrection.

Equally isolated is the figure of Jacob Epstein, whom I
have already described as an expressionist – again, a label
the artist himself would probably disown. His work, as is
well known, falls into two distinct divisions – portraits
that are a development of the Renaissance tradition which
we associate with the work of a sculptor like Donatello, and
monumental subjects that at one time betrayed a tendency
to abstraction (the Oscar Wilde memorial, for example)
and which always seem ready to free themselves from
naturalistic conventions. But these two styles, distinct in
their extremes, actually coalesce, and from *Genesis* to
Lazarus there is a gradual infusion of would-be abstract
forms with violent emotional content; whereas some of the

portrait busts (*Joseph Conrad*, for example) carry th
psychological revelation to an expressionist degree
caricature (caricature being a persistent type of exp
sionist art). There has never been a retrospective exhib
of Epstein's work on a grand scale, and there has be
tendency among critics (of which I feel guilty myself) t
his achievement apart, as something which might be
with as a separate issue, but which is essentially irreleva
the main development of art in our time. This is no
unusual phenomenon in the history of culture – we m
compare the position, in literature, of an isolated figure l
Charles Doughty, or even Thomas Hardy. We might s
that there are exiles of spirit as well as of place, and only
time will gather them to the fold.

I have described expressionism as the characteristic style
of the Northern latitudes, but though there may be significant shades of difference, it is also the characteristic style
of the Jews, and Epstein in this respect has affinities with
artists like Chagall, Soutine and Kisling. But when that
superficial observation has been made, it must be admitted
that there is a more essential relation to the work of
Rouault, who is the son of a Breton father and a Parisian
mother, and therefore well within our Northern latitudes.
These generalizations, therefore, can only be put forward
with great diffidence. It is perhaps more important to observe that the expressionistic style of Rouault has given
him the same kind of isolation in France that Epstein and
Stanley Spencer have 'enjoyed' in England.

To understand the reason for our curious isolation from
the general trend of northern art, we must go back some
centuries in our history. In the Middle Ages there is no
evidence of detachment: indeed, for some centuries England was a prime source of plastic invention, and contributed her full share to the formation and evolution of the
Gothic style. In England we like to think that this contribution included some elements of unique value – a linear
grace such as we find in the illustrations to the Lindisfarne

Gospels, and a lyricism which is the distinctive character of our cathedral architecture.

The general character of English Gothic art cannot be described as expressionistic, though it has expressionistic phases, notably in some schools of manuscript illumination, alabaster carving and stained-glass painting. In that respect it is neither more nor less expressionistic than northern art in general, and though we did not produce a masterpiece of expressionistic painting like Mathias Grünewald's *Crucifixion*, there is plenty of evidence of an art of the same general character. But what I would like to emphasize in the present connexion is that the whole of this native English art, expressionist or not, was destined suddenly to disappear. Early in the sixteenth century a blight descended on our painting and sculpture: our aesthetic sensibility seemed to become atrophied, our instinct for plastic form disappeared, or was evident only in domestic architecture, or in the minor arts of the silversmith and the furniture-maker. This aesthetic blackout lasted for about three centuries – until, early in the nineteenth century, our slumbering sensibility was reawakened, and found expression in the geniuses of Constable, Bonington and Turner.

During the three centuries of our aesthetic blackout, there was art in England, but it was largely an imported art – the art of Holbein and Van Dyck in painting, of Italian and Dutch architects and sculptors, of German musicians. Various ideological and sociological explanations can be given of the internal weakness in this country which made such a cultural invasion inevitable, but it is the technical aspect of the process that is of greatest interest in the present context. Our early art, in common with the style diffused through the whole of northern Europe, was linear – that is to say, it was a two-dimensional and geometrical art. But the arts which developed in Europe during the Renaissance were three-dimensional, based on the discovery of methods, to which the technique of oil-painting lent itself, of representing perspective and space. The English artists could not absorb this technical advance: either they were not clever enough, or there was some psychological inhibition in our isolated northern nature. English patrons, however, who belonged to the international *élite* of court and aristocracy, insisted on being in the fashion, and began to import the new art of the south. The linear art of England still lingered on in miniature painting, in architecture and the crafts, but it was a tenuous existence and easily succumbed to those negative forces represented by Puritanism. Thanks to Puritanism, which associated the plastic arts with royalism and Roman Catholicism, art in England acquired that suggestion of immorality and ultramontanism from which it perhaps still suffers a little. For three centuries the plastic arts in England were to be treated as imported luxuries, like port and sherry.

If we add to that stylistic explanation the vast material factors which spring from the Industrial Revolution, we begin to have an adequate picture of the losing battle which our artists were compelled to fight. The Industrial Revolution created those purely materialistic values which found their characteristic expression, not in the arts, but in the empire – in mass-production, trade expansion, and the ideal of comfort. The evolution of Puritanism and the evolution of capitalist industry are not unconnected, as historians like Max Weber and R. H. Tawney have shown: and, from our point of view, these forces combined to destroy the social basis of art. The individual artist in an industrial society such as England was henceforth a social outcast, a misfit. He might exist on the aristocratic fringe, and by prostituting his talents; but at best he was but a deformed creature, like Hogarth and Cruikshank, turning his native linear genius into the channels of satire and caricature; or, like Blake, a lonely and isolated genius, condemned to a lifetime of poverty and neglect.

In the second half of the eighteenth century and the first part of the nineteenth, there was that brief expansion of a painterly art which gave us the considerable figures of

Gainsborough and Constable, and a whole school of water-colourists and landscape painters culminating in the great genius of Turner. There was still a conflict between innate gifts and foreign fashions, and this conflict was expressed in some tragic failures – the failure of Romney, for example, who had not the courage to be English; the failure of Reynolds who had the delusive ambition to be classical. Blake, more conscious than any of his contemporaries of the real nature of plastic inspiration, said that Reynolds was 'hired by Satan to depress art'. What is common to Constable and Turner is a conscious rejection of the classical ideals which obscured whatever native genius there was in Romney and Reynolds: and a return to nature, to nature in the sense of the English landscape, a return which involved an honest attempt to render the sensations experienced in the observation of nature. Incidentally, a similar process was taking place in English poetry, which culminated in the genius of Wordsworth, and the whole aesthetic sentiment of this period may be studied as a unified phenomenon – poet and painter alike responded to some subtle change of mentality. This new development – when it reached its highest point, in the late work of Turner – was once more fully expressionistic. Though Turner was to be a source of inspiration to the impressionists, his late work goes beyond impressionism, which always has an objective sense of reality, to make the work of art a symbol of the artist's inner or subjective feelings. The late landscapes of Turner actually anticipate by nearly a century the landscapes of expressionist painters like Munch and Kokoschka.

I have digressed from my main subject, but I may now be able to explain more clearly than would otherwise have been possible certain new phases of English painting and sculpture. Again I must be severely selective in my choice of examples, confining myself to certain representative figures. It will be convenient to begin with Graham Sutherland.

Graham Sutherland (born 1903) is certainly a painter

fully aware of the complex development of modern art on the Continent. If he has evolved his own style, it is not in deliberate isolation from the School of Paris. But he has his deepest roots in the native tradition – in that tradition which was reanimated by William Blake, Samuel Palmer (a follower of Blake whose early work has recently been redis-covered), and Turner. Like Palmer and Turner he is an artist who begins with the observation of landscape, but the end result, which might well be related to Turner's expres-sionist phase, is much farther removed from naturalistic conventions than any work of Palmer's. Though he always has an object in nature to inspire him, in the process of 'translation' which follows, Sutherland evolves a composi-tion in which the object is often no longer recognizable. It would not be true to say that the result is then 'abstract', because the forms which remain in the picture are still recognizably *organic*. Sutherland selects particular aspects in landscape – it might be, in his own words, 'the twisted gorse on the cliff edge or twigs, like snakes, lying on the path, the bare rock, worn, and showing through the path, heath fires . . . gorse burnt and blackened after fire . . . the high overhanging hedges by the steep road which pinch the setting sun . . . mantling clouds against a black sky and the thunder . . . the deep green valleys and the rounded hills and the whole structure, simple and complex . . .' But hav-ing selected his subject, it seemed to the artist impossible to sit down and make finished drawings from nature : in-deed, there were no ready-made subjects to paint: the reality was elsewhere, in the painter's mind. 'The essence was intellectual and emotional.' And so the painter found that he could express what he felt only by paraphrasing what he saw. His paintings, therefore, are a transmutation of natural facts, faithful to the sensational reality of the moment when these facts were first registered in the painter's consciousness.

Sutherland is primarily a landscape artist, and it is but rarely that he gives a human scale to his compositions by the

4. DAVID JONES:
The Gentle Bird. 1950

inclusion of a figure. But his most important work to date, a *Crucifixion* commissioned in 1946 for the church of St Matthew, Northampton, is an abrupt departure from his familiar subject-matter, and, indeed, a significant event in the history of contemporary English painting. It is significant in the first place because it is an attempt to use the idioms of modern art in the service of the Christian tradition. It is significant, too, because the quality which such a challenge has evoked is more decisively expressionistic than any example of English art that I know. There remain in the composition certain elements of other styles which do not seem to me to be fully integrated – a somewhat arbitrary suggestion of cubism in the representation of the Cross, and certain symbolic accessories in the lower part of the composition which do not immediately make an emotional impact. This stylistic hesitation reflects the dilemma which faces the modern artist whenever he is called upon to communicate general ideas, or objective facts – it is the same dilemma that Picasso had to face in painting his *Guernica*. Generally speaking, modern art is a personalist art, subjective in its origins and arbitrary in its conventions. It has never, hitherto, aspired to be a monumental art, a public art used in public rituals. It must necessarily undergo certain modifications if it is to become a functional art in this sense.

A less equivocal example of Sutherland's figure painting is his recent (1950) portrait of Somerset Maugham. A certain symbolic transformation still takes place, notably in the monolithic presentation of the subject and in the handling of such details as the folds and creases of the clothing; but for a parallel we should have to go to early expressionistic portraits by Kokoschka or Otto Dix.

Sutherland would disclaim any intention of leading a new school, but a number of younger painters, by virtue of the general character of their work, can be grouped round him. John Minton and John Craxton, for example, have paraphrased landscape very much in the same spirit as Sutherland. Keith Vaughan and Michael Ayrton, in both landscape and figure subjects, belong to the same development, though Ayrton, in his most recent work, seems to be cultivating a more romantic type of symbolism.

That the new trends in contemporary English art are not confined to landscape is shown by a painter like Robert Colquhoun. Colquhoun is a Scotsman, born in 1914, one of several young artists from that country who are beginning to make an impression on the general public, but his artistic origins are not provincial. He owes something to the general post-cubist tradition, and, like some of the younger painters in Paris to-day, he seems to be attempting a new synthesis, based on the diverse movements of the past forty years. He owes something, perhaps unconsciously, to the Celtic love of complicated linear designs, but essentially he adopts towards the human figure the same attitude as Sutherland adopts to landscape – that is to say, he takes the intellectual and emotional essence of the subject and para- phrases it into an expressive design. His figures are fantastic, inhabitants of a dream world, and yet they still belong to the organic world: they are alive and individual: they have the vitality of the idols of some animistic cult. Colquhoun's paintings also possess a very characteristic colour scheme, generally controlled within a narrow range of reds and browns and giving perfect emphasis to the concentrated power of the composition. Colquhoun has also experimented with a graphic technique called 'monotype', and in this medium his work betrays a close affinity with similar graphic work of the German Expressionists and Rouault. The same is true of the work of his friend and fellow- Scotsman, Robert MacBryde. A few years ago MacBryde was painting still-life compositions in the tradition of the Paris School, but his recent work belongs to the same ex- pressionist style as Colquhoun's. It is possible to detect in these latest paintings of Colquhoun and MacBryde, as well as in the work of a young painter from Ireland, Louis Le Brocquy, the influence of Jankel Adler, an expressionist painter who came to England as a refugee in the early days of the war.

There are several other painters who could be included in this expressionist development – Francis Bacon, although his work gives an extra 'frisson' which might be called surrealistic, and Edward Burra, although his fantasy is more free and 'poetic' than in expressionism generally. Even so subtle a painter as Ivon Hitchens, devoid as his style is of any suggestion of dogmatic intention, is essentially expressionistic, translating the sensational impact of landscape into free plastic harmonies of almost luminous colour.* Even the landscapes of John Piper, though they may be controlled by a conscious desire to make a topographical record of the scene or building, are generally inspissated with a romantic melancholy which is essentially expressionistic.

We must presently consider this new development in British painting in relation to other and quite opposite trends, but before we do this there is an artist whose work is not so readily fitted into the expressionistic niche, and is nevertheless not so far removed from some of the superficial appearances of that style – I refer to Henry Moore. Preoccupied as he is with the human form, it is still possible to say that his attitude towards nature is the same as Graham Sutherland's – he paraphrases what he sees in order to express what he feels. In the art of sculpture, however, a greater spiritual and, indeed, physical effort is needed to effect such a transformation. There is not the same possibility of improvisation as in painting, and I think that as a consequence Henry Moore has had to carry what one might

* 'Free plastic harmonies' is a question-begging phrase, for how can harmony, which is the product of mathematical quantities, be free? My meaning, beautifully illustrated by the paintings of Ivon Hitchens, is that the painter, taking his formal structure from nature, then infuses it with expressive colour. 'The essence of my theory', writes this artist (in a letter to the author), 'is that colour is space and space is colour, and these must be right as well as the two-dimensional pattern. Therefore, if my rendering is correct, the picture will look true in depth and natural, though not naturalistic.' The difference between the 'natural' and the 'naturalistic' is due to the artist's personal vision (or his sensational reactions, to use more scientific language); that is to say, to the expressive or 'expressionistic' element in his painting.

call his animistic philosophy a stage further than any of his contemporaries. I use this word 'animistic', because Henry Moore, in common with artists of his type throughout the ages, would seem to believe that behind the appearance of things there is some kind of transcendental energy, a will to form, which is only partially revealed in organic life. Those actual forms are, as it were, expedients determined by the haphazard circumstances of time and place, the struggle for existence or for power. The artist must try to identify himself with this immanent will to form, and strive to express the particular shape that such a force would create in a given emotional situation. But the artist can arrive at an intuition of such forms only by close study of the forms actually evolved in the phenomenal world. Henry Moore has based his sculpture on such a close observation of natural forms. As a student he drew and modelled from life for many years, and he still periodically returns to life drawing. But in his sculpture Moore does not draw directly upon the memory or observations of a particular object, but rather uses whatever comes up from his general fund of knowledge of natural forms.

That is to say, the artist like Moore by means of his drawings makes himself so familiar with the ways of nature – particularly the ways of growth – that he can out of the depth and sureness of that knowledge create forms which have all the vital rhythm and structure of natural forms. In the particular case of a reclining figure carved in wood, a knowledge of the organic structure of the material enables the artist to use the peculiarities of that structure to emphasize the corresponding organic forms of the human figure. The 'contours' that appear in a cross-section of a tree-trunk, due to the 'rings' of annual growth, can be used to suggest the contours of bulging forms of bones and muscles. It may be said, therefore (to use a formula I have used elsewhere in this connexion), that *the aim of a sculptor like Henry Moore is to represent his conceptions in forms natural to the material he is working in*.

28

Such a formula is deceptive if it leads to the assumption that Moore's sculpture is in some sense 'automatic'. Every great artist depends on certain formal intuitions. In addition to expressing or representing a concept (reclining figure, mother and child, etc.), he has to endow his creation with life, with its own innate vitality. This is a question of physical relationships (mass, space, rhythm, proportions, etc.). Vitality in organic objects is an effect of movement – either the immediate movements of muscles, or the slow movement of growth. The sculptor's problem is to give this dynamic quality to objects which do not move or grow. It is done by establishing certain relations between a solid mass and its surrounding space, and by dividing the mass into contrasted areas, convexities and concavities which are rhythmically related and *seem* to move into one another. To create such vitality in an inanimate mass is an infinitely difficult task, and only the greatest sculptors have been capable of it. It demands not only a particular kind of plastic sensibility, but in addition the capacity to translate this sensibility into objective material form. It is difficult enough to achieve an integrated harmony of this kind with a fixed point of view (the painter's problem); it demands far greater powers of formal organization to achieve the same degree of integration in a work of art than can be observed from multiple points of view.

It is important to realize that the figures which Moore carves according to these principles are never, strictly speaking, symbolic. Therefore he never gives his sculptures literary titles; they are always 'figures', 'compositions', or simply particular and individual existences – a mother and child, never Maternity. The nearest he has come to a symbolic content is in the *Madonna and Child* which was commissioned for the same church in Northampton as Sutherland's *Crucifixion*. The qualities which the sculptor tries to express in such a work, destined for a specifically Christian function (qualities which Moore himself has described as 'austerity', 'grandeur', 'quiet dignity and

29

gentleness', 'complete easiness and repose') are all qualities which can be immediately related to formal values; to angles and geometrical proportions. In other words, every intellectual value or emotional tone must be given an aesthetic justification, and that involves the dilemma which I have already described in referring to Sutherland's *Crucifixion*. In the *Madonna and Child* there is a certain restraint which is not strictly aesthetic. There is a certain conscription of the artist's powers: freedom is sacrificed to function.

We return to the question already posed: Can the work of Henry Moore be included within the same expressionistic trend as Colquhoun's and Sutherland's? It certainly bears the same relation to the natural world – it is not a 'realization' of the appearance of that world such as Cézanne attempted and such as underlies the whole classical tradition: it is, to use Sutherland's word again, a *paraphrase* of that world: it is that world as refracted through the emotions of the artist. It may be that Moore confines himself to the representation of a more elementary but at the same time more essential aspect of the object: many of his figures are surcharged with what one can only call a certain primitive animism. They invite what the anthropologists call *participation mystique* rather than detached admiration. That is to say, the spectator merges his vital and sympathetic feelings in the life of the object contemplated. From another point of view we might say that Moore's carvings are nearer to Saxon stone-carvings and Romanesque art generally than to later types of northern art; and their relation to Mexican art, and even to certain phases of the art of Picasso, is also evident. But it would be a mistake to conclude from these superficial resemblances or admitted influences that the work of Moore was merely eclectic. It is rather the most fully integrated and authentically personal art of our time. The art of Henry Moore is certainly far removed from the tradition represented by French sculptors like Rodin and Maillol. It represents a decisive new departure in the evolution of modern sculpture, and it is this originality that makes one hesitate to apply to it a label so charged with historical significance as 'expressionist'. But there are certain drawings which Moore made during the war in the bomb shelters of London which reveal clearly enough an essentially expressionistic quality in his work, and that part of his work which is definitely not expressionistic, the calm humanism of the *Madonna and Child* or the intellectual abstraction of certain carvings of 1935–7, is inconsiderable in proportion to the whole of his work.

I must now mention a third group of contemporary English artists who cannot by any means be fitted into the expressionistic trend. The general character of their work is non-figurative, or non-representational. It is true that in certain types of this so-called 'abstract' art, one can still discern vague reminiscences of the human figure or of landscape, as in the work of John Tunnard. But at the extreme of abstraction, as in certain works of Ben Nicholson and Barbara Hepworth, there is no longer any reference to the phenomenal world, the world of appearance. A completely new order of reality is created, and the result has to be appreciated with the kind of faculties we normally reserve for non-representational arts like music and architecture. Art of this type has close affinities with the work of various Continental painters and sculptors. Nicholson, for example, began painting in the tradition of Braque, Picasso and Juan Gris, and was later decisively influenced by Piet Mondrian. But working in recent years in relative isolation, he has pursued a consistent trend towards an art of absolute form. Endowed with a sensibility for structural relations and colour harmonies of the greatest refinement, he has produced a series of works which avoid the sterile academism of so much abstract art and constitute one of the most considerable achievements in English painting of to-day. He has carried the practice of abstraction to its logical extreme, where the art of painting becomes as pure and absolute as the art of music. This art has met with almost universal

31

resistance in England, not only from the public, but even from those critics and fellow-painters who cannot be accused of conservatism. And this is understandable when we realize the decisive nature of the break which such paintings make with every convention of pictorial art. The art of Picasso, for example, always retains some contact with the organic world, the world of appearances. But the characteristic art of Ben Nicholson or Barbara Hepworth has no connexion with the world of appearances: its origins are within the mind and sensitive organism of the artist, and it does not depend for its values on any reference to the external world, unless it be to the basic formal structures of physical and biological phenomena. Its values are the self-contained values of concrete harmony, of balance, rhythm and inner coherence. Such art can be appreciated only by some faculty analogous to that with which we appreciate the music of Bach: it requires us to develop, on the visual side, what we have without protest developed on the aural side.

To attempt to create such an art in tri-dimensional form is a natural step to take, once the underlying principle has been admitted. Here again we are familiar with sculpture which has an abstract tendency – the work of Laurens, Arp, Brancusi, Giacometti, for example; but in all such work there is usually, as in the paintings of Picasso, or the sculpture of Henry Moore, an organic germ, or a reference, however remote, to organic forms. Such sculpture has now reached a stage of pure plasticity wholly comparable with the paintings of Mondrian or Nicholson. It is at this extreme of experimental development that we find the work of Barbara Hepworth, very tense, very sensitive, and completely integrated within its world of pure form.

Nothing is more astonishing, in contemporary art, than the persistence of this abstract style in the face of the obliquity of critics and the indifference of the general public. It would almost seem as if the artist, possessed by some unconscious collective force, was driven to express a reaction against all that is organic and naturalistic. When a

5. ROBERT MACBRYDE:
Table in a Red Room. 1950

distinguished and successful naturalistic painter like Victor Pasmore abandons his naturalism to become an abstract painter, one cannot believe that he is responding to any public demand, or that his motives are even reasonably prudent. His conversion is more 'mystical', and there is a certain suggestion of sacrifice and asceticism about the whole movement. It may be explained as an unconscious reaction to the social instability of the world in which the artist finds himself; and it would not be difficult to find parallel developments in philosophy and religion. Whatever the profounder explanation of the movement, there can be no doubt of its vitality and aesthetic validity. The expansion of the movement abroad, in America and on the Continent, is even more remarkable than it has been in Great Britain; but even in this country the proportion of artists of abstract tendency is considerable, particularly among the sculptors. Here the influence of the Constructivist movement is evident, and an explanation can be found in the fact that the leading constructivist sculptor, Naum Gabo, was recently resident in England for a number of years.

The rise of a native school of sculpture in Great Britain is of unusual significance, for it is centuries since this art counted for anything in this country. The influence of Henry Moore is the most obvious explanation of the phenomenon, but some of the younger sculptors – Butler and Paolozzi, to mention two of the most original of them – do not owe everything to Moore, and, by developing a 'linear' convention, may be said to be far away from Moore's essentially massive vision. Linear sculpture, the outlining of space and the representation of rhythm by means of wires and rods, is a new departure in the plastic arts, deriving from Giacometti and Picasso, but developed independently in various new directions by Calder in America, Butler, Paolozzi, Turnbull, and Chadwick in England, and by Hans Uhlmann in Germany. Its potentialities are yet to be fully exploited.

There are two further tendencies in contemporary art in

E*   33

Great Britain which should be mentioned, though neither can be said to constitute an active and coherent group. The break-up of the Surrealist Movement as a direct consequence of the Second World War is an historical event which has never yet been adequately explained, but as it is a question that mainly concerns other countries, it would be out of place to discuss it now. I would only observe that it was, in the first place, a physical dispersion. The leading personalities of the movement had maintained a revolutionary attitude in the pre-war period, and this made it necessary for them to flee from the Nazi tyranny. What requires explanation is the continuing failure of the movement to reconstitute itself after the war. This is a complicated problem not unconnected with the general political disillusionment that took place during the war – for there was always a close connexion between surrealism and communism. But in England, for reasons which I have discussed elsewhere, surrealism never crystallized into an independent group of a distinct character – most of our surrealists kept a foot in some other camp, and never fully committed themselves to that 'automatism' of creative activity which André Breton has always made the criterion of a surrealist attitude in art. Francis Bacon, though he has never, to my knowledge, called himself a surrealist, is probably the most consistent surrealist among us. Others who might claim the title are too consciously fantastic. Nevertheless there are characteristics in the art of painters like John Armstrong, Francis Bacon, Edward Burra, Robert Colquhoun, Merlyn Evans, Tristram Hillier, Louis le Brocquy, Roland Penrose, Robert MacBryde, Ceri Richards, Julian Trevelyan, John Tunnard, Keith Vaughan, and Bryan Wynter, and sculptors like Adams, Butler, Chadwick, and McWilliam which, given coherence and scope, might have constituted a vigorous surrealist movement in England.* That this did not happen

---

*A 'déclaration du groupe surréaliste en Angleterre' was contributed to *Le Surréalisme en* 1947 (Paris, Maeght) and carried fourteen signatures, but further manifestations of this group in England itself have not been in evidence.

34

was due to anti-organizational traits in the English character rather than to any absence of appropriate talent.

The other tendency which might be said to have petered out is the politically inspired school of socialist realism. There was a time when it seemed possible that a group would be formed within the politically orientated Artists International Association, but it never became coherent enough to produce any outstanding artists. It is an independent painter like L. S. Lowry, patiently elaborating his talent in the provinces, who has given us the most realistic picture of the life of industrial workers in this country.

There are several other artists who remain independent of groups and tendencies. The delicate lyrical sensibility of David Jones or Mary Kessel; the objective naturalism of Lucian Freud; and distinct from these many individual talents of grace and charm, justified in their activity, giving insight or interest to the routine of our lives, but not pretending to that more-than-personal significance which reflects some deeper movement of the human spirit.

There is no doubt that a longing for a return to naturalism is often felt by a public not conscious of the artist's problem. Actually there are two publics. One, numerically the larger, thinks of the painter as the provider of a commodity that it is seeking; and what this public seeks is a confirmation of its own world, of its own bourgeois values. The other and smaller public realizes that the great artist, the artist who in the end is going to give it most satisfaction, is looking beyond the present, trying to find a stepping-stone into the uncertain future. The more uncertain that future is — and it has never been so uncertain as it is to-day — the more desperate will be the plunge forward, and there will always be the risk of disaster. But it can be nothing comparable to the disaster to be experienced by those people who one day will find that their world of conventional values has disappeared, and that they are left in a maddening chaos. Reality is not the four walls of the room we are sitting in, or the trees and men we see out of our window; it is a mental construction, a stability of vision, and the next phase of human development may find such stability in an art that is anti-organic, absolute, and ideal. It has happened before in the history of the world and it may happen again.*

This abstract development may seem to have taken us far from that general return to native tradition which, at the beginning of this essay, I gave as the most general characteristic of our art to-day. But it might be argued that a painter like Ben Nicholson has retreated even more violently into the past, for the nearest analogy to his geometrical abstractions is to be found in the formal ornament of our Celtic manuscripts. I do not believe that Ben Nicholson himself is conscious of any such resemblance, or is in any sense a reactionary artist. But it is possible that art has a certain

---

*I would like to quote from the correspondence columns of *The Listener* (3 August 1950) an extract from a letter written by one of our most subtle naturalistic painters. It expresses with great perceptiveness the significance of abstract art in our time. Mr David Jones wrote:

'Those of us whose work no one, I imagine, would call "abstract", know, nevertheless, that it is an abstract *quality*, however hidden or devious, which determines the real worth of any work. This is true of Botticelli's Primavera, of the White Horse of Uffington, of the music of Monteverdi, of *Finnegans Wake*, of the "Alfred jewel", of the glass goblet I am now trying to draw, of the shape of a liturgy, of the shape of a tea-cup. The one common factor implicit in all the arts of man resides in a certain juxtaposing of forms.

'In theory "abstract art" is no more than a conscious assertion of this truth. It is then the assertion, in isolation, of a real, and indeed a first, principle. The least "abstract" work (in the contemporary sense) could not be made apart from this principle, for without it a "thing" having integration and a life of its own, could not be. Therefore without it the arts could not be. With this clearly understood we may then be in a better position to consider what possible aridities or impoverishments may or may not attend, or be latent in, the practice of what is called "pure abstraction" among us to-day. That is a real and interesting issue and a totally impersonal one.

'Like much else, it is best considered in its historical setting, e.g. why has a certain preoccupation with the "abstract" marked much of the painting of our day? It is certainly no accident. It is a complex matter, but this we can say, that whatever vacuities and banalities have accompanied this preoccupation, it has also been directly responsible for works of real creativity, and indirectly has influenced to this or that degree most of the more vital work of our time. Remembering that our time is that of a "late civilization", in which severe stress as to what direction is bound to be the lot of most serious artists, Blake's poignant and apposite question, "Do you, sir, paint in fear and trembling?" might also be asked of critics with regard to their trade.'

relationship to magic, or, to express the idea in more fashionable terms, it is possible that the artist, in the degree that he achieves an integration of his personality through the medium of art, does so by making contact with those forces which Freud has called man's archaic heritage, and which Jung has called the collective unconscious. In a world of prevailing insecurity and inhumanity a retreat into the realm of pure form is, as I have already said, not only a natural reaction, but also a necessary revolution.

These considerations lead to the posing of a dilemma which the protagonist of contemporary art has no wish to evade. His antagonist will argue in this way: The world, you admit, is in a sad state – civilization such as the nineteenth century conceived it is visibly disintegrating, and in this period of painful transition, art itself can only be transitional. Granted that the art of our time is true to the material and spiritual conditions of our time, these conditions are so basically unsound, insecure, and ephemeral that we may surely regard the art that reflects them as sick and degenerate, and certainly of no lasting value.

So argued Hitler and Goebbels; but so argue also many honest minds that would hate to find themselves in such company – timid conservatives, prejudiced academicians, frightened politicians, and a great body of simple but puzzled people.

To all such critics of modern art we must answer, in the first place, that in the world of art to touch pitch is not necessarily to be defiled. Great works of art in other ages have been inspired by gruesome and filthy subjects – slaughter and torture, dead carcasses and hideous human beings. But that is not the point, our critics will argue: we have no objection to war and revolution, neurosis and despair, *as subjects*; but you must paint them *beautifully*, just as Leonardo and Rembrandt did. If Picasso's *Guernica* had been painted in the same style as the Anghiari battle-piece, why then we should know how to react!

So it is a question of form, not of content. The critics of

modern art want their wine (and very sour wine it is) in old bottles. To this we can only reply that the mind of the artist does not work in that way, and never has worked in that way except in decadent periods. Original experience provokes its unique form. The whole history of art demonstrates, with utmost clarity, that the particular emotions and particular outlook of a period always seek to find their particular forms of expression. Similarities exist between the forms of similar phases of history, but as history never repeats itself exactly, such forms of art remain similarities, and are not identities.

It is part of the business of the art critic to search for such similarities, and in this essay I have tried to make some comparisons between the formal aspects of modern English art and the art of certain past phases of English art. It is only in this sense that one speaks of a 'revival' of art, or of Great Britain 'making a definite contribution to the cultural revival of Western Europe'. To speak of a 'revival' of culture at the present stage of social transition is perhaps to be imprecisely optimistic; but any spiritual or intellectual movement that faithfully reflects the stresses and conflicts of modern society is to that extent positive and progressive. In any case, a cultural revival will not, in my opinion, be achieved by a specifically European movement in the arts, concentrated on Paris, or Moscow, or any other centre. The cultural unity we all desire as the basis of political unity will be artificial and insecure unless it is a focus of the diversity and multiplicity of local and individual forces. Unity is not the spiritual counterpart of uniformity, and each country will contribute most to the unity we all desire by exploiting its own idiosyncrasies, and by remaining true to the traditions which have become a part of its character and destiny. We are prepared to admit with Kipling that 'East is East and West is West, and never the twain shall meet'; but this observation might have been made with equal justice of the north and the south. We cannot escape our mental climates, for they are in a literal sense the creation of our prevailing winds and the chemistry of our soils. It is inconceivable that English art should be *decisively* influenced by Indian art, or French art by African art. In saying this I am fully conscious of such cross currents as the influence of Negro sculpture on Picasso (though Picasso himself refuses to attach any special importance to this influence), or the influence of Mexican sculpture on Henry Moore. Such influences are like injections of a drug: they act as a temporary stimulus and restore the body to health. I do not deny their necessity or deprecate their usefulness. But they are shocks which should be absorbed into the main bloodstream: they should not persist as a habit or a fashion. The history of art shows that the art of any particular region always tends to revert to a regional norm – to a mode of sensibility and style of expression determined, we must assume, by ethnic and geographic factors. There is no need to base a philosophy, much less a religion, on such simple materialistic premises. Art cannot be confined within frontiers – it lives only if continually subjected to foreign invasions, to migrations and transplantations. But if art's vitality comes from the cross-breeding of styles, its strength comes from stability, from roots that grow deep into a native soil. The typical style of northern Europe alternates between abstraction and expressionism. We may for a time successfully absorb the style of southern Europe, and we have had idealistic and naturalistic artists of great talent. But our natural talent lies elsewhere – in those styles which spring from introspective and personalistic moods. Such styles are in both the critical and historical sense romantic by nature: the genius of our greatest painters and architects no less than of our greatest poets was always romantic. In that sense the general trend of contemporary art may be interpreted as a return to our romantic tradition.

NOTES ON THE ARTISTS

ROBERT ADAMS. Born at Northampton, 1917. Northampton School of Art. Teacher at the Central School of Art, London. (Plate 59)

LEONARD APPLEBEE. Born in London, 1911. Goldsmiths' College School of Art and the Royal College of Art. (Plate 23)

JOHN ARMSTRONG. Born at Hastings, Sussex, in 1893. St John's Wood School of Art, London. Besides painting he has designed costumes, etc., for numerous films, theatre productions, and ballet. He served in the Army throughout the First World War, and was an official war artist during the Second. (Plate 32)

MICHAEL AYRTON. Born in London, 1921. Heatherley's and St John's Wood School of Art, London, and in Paris. With John Minton he designed the costumes and décor for John Gielgud's production of *Macbeth* in 1942, and in 1944 he designed the ballet *Le Festin de l'Araignée* for the Sadler's Wells Company. Art critic of *The Spectator* 1944 to 1946. (Plate 43)

FRANCIS BACON. Born in Dublin, 1910. (Plate 64)

WILHELMINA BARNS-GRAHAM. Born at St Andrews, 1912. Edinburgh College of Art, October, 1931–6. Awarded postgraduate travelling scholarship 1937. (Plate 52)

EDWARD BAWDEN. Born at Braintree, Essex, 1903. Cambridge School of Art and (1922) the Royal College of Art. During the Second World War, an official war artist in France, the Middle East. In 1946 was made a C.B.E., and in 1947 an A.R.A. (Plate 13)

EDWARD BURRA. Born in London, 1905. Chelsea School of Art and the Royal College of Art. Travelled in Europe and the United States. He was a member of Unit One and has exhibited with the English Surrealists. Besides painting in water-colour he designs scenery and costumes for ballet. (Plate 36)

REG BUTLER. Born 1913. Trained as an architect. R.I.B.A. (1937). (Plate 60)

LYNN CHADWICK. Born in London, 1914. Trained as an architect. (Plate 63)

PRUNELLA CLOUGH. Born in London, 1919. Studied at Chelsea School of Art 1937–9. (Plate 31)

6. GRAHAM SUTHERLAND: Standing Form. 1950

WILLIAM COLDSTREAM. Born at Belford, Northumberland, 1908. Slade School, London, 1926–9; became a member of the London Group, 1933; in association with Claude Rogers and Victor Pasmore founded the Euston Road School of Drawing and Painting, 1937. Served with the Royal Engineers throughout the Second World War, for the last two years as an official war artist in the Middle East and Italy. Since 1949 Slade Professor of Fine Art at University College, London. (Plate 5)

ROBERT COLQUHOUN. Born at Kilmarnock, Ayrshire, 1914. Glasgow School of Art, 1933–8. Travelled in Italy, France, Holland, and Belgium. (Plate 48)

JOHN CRAXTON. Born in London, 1922. Goldsmiths' College School of Art and Westminster School of Art. (Plate 46)

ALAN DAVIE. Born at Grangemouth, Scotland 1920. Edinburgh College of Art (Andrew Grant Scholarship), Guthrie Award, Royal Scottish Academy, 1941. Studied in France, Switzerland, Italy, Sicily, Spain, 1948–9. (Plate 27)

ROY DE MAISTRE. Born in Australia in 1898 of French descent. First exhibited in New South Wales in 1917, in England for the first time in the Royal Academy of 1922. Awarded the Society of Artists Travelling Scholarship in 1923 and exhibited in the Paris Salon of 1924. (Plate 37)

FRANK DOBSON. Born 1889. Professor of Sculpture, Royal College of Art. An Associate of the Royal Academy. (Plate 45)

H. E. DU PLESSIS. Born in the Transvaal in 1894. During the First World War served in Africa and the Middle East. Over thirty when he began painting, without art school training. Member of the London Group. (Plate 12)

JACOB EPSTEIN. Born in New York, 1880. Paris (École des Beaux Arts, Académie Julian). (Plate 2)

MERLYN EVANS. Born in Cardiff, 1910. Glasgow School of Art, 1925–30. Royal College of Art, 1930–2. Paris, Berlin, Copenhagen and Italy. Lived in South Africa, 1937–40. During the war served in the Eighth Army in North Africa and Italy. Exhibited at the International Exhibition of Surrealism (1936) at the New Burlington Galleries, London. (Plate 51)

LUCIAN FREUD. Born 1922. Goldsmiths' College School of Art. (Plate 8)

WILLIAM GEAR. Born in Scotland, 1915. Edinburgh College

of Art, 1932–7. Europe, 1937–8. War service, 1940–7. Worked in Paris till 1950. (Plate 54)

W. G. GILLIES. Born 1898. Edinburgh College of Art, with further study in Paris and Italy. A member of the Society of Scottish Artists, the 1922 Group and the Society of Eight. Elected an Associate of the Royal Society of Artists in 1940. (Plate 15)

LAWRENCE GOWING. Born at Stoke Newington, London, 1918. Studied at Euston Road School. Member of London Group. Professor of Fine Art at the University of Durham since 1948. (Plate 4)

STANLEY WILLIAM HAYTER. Born in London, 1901. King's College, London (B.Sc. Hons. Chemistry); Research Chemist, Anglo-Iranian Oil Co, 1922–5. Founded Atelier 17, Paris, 1927; U.S.A. 1940–9; now directs Atelier 17 in Paris again. (Plate 53)

BARBARA HEPWORTH. Born at Wakefield, Yorkshire, 1903. Leeds School of Art, Royal College of Art. Travelling scholarship, Italy, 1924. (Plate 56)

PATRICK HERON. Born at Headingley, Leeds, 1920. Lived at St Ives, Cornwall, 1925–30. Slade School of Art, 1937–9. Art critic of the *New Statesman and Nation*, 1947–50. Designs textiles for Cresta Silks, Ltd. (Plate 30)

TRISTRAM HILLIER. Born in Peking, 1905. The Slade School, London, and Paris. Except during the war of 1939–45 he has lived chiefly in France, especially at Dieppe. (Plate 19)

IVON HITCHENS. Born in London, 1893. St John's Wood School of Art and the Royal Academy Schools. Member of the Seven and Five Society, the London Group, and the Society of Mural Painters. (Colour Plate 3)

AUGUSTUS JOHN, O.M. Born at Tenby, Wales, 1878. The Slade School of Art. Member of the New English Art Club. Professor at the Liverpool Academy, 1901–2. Elected a Royal Academician in 1928. Subsequently resigned and re-elected 1940. President of the Society of Mural Painters. (Plate 1)

DAVID JONES. Born at Brockley, Kent, 1895. Camberwell School of Art and Westminster School of Art. From 1922–6 he lived mostly with Eric Gill, and under that sculptor's tuition he learned the techniques of wood and copper engraving. In

42

1938 won the Hawthornden Prize for Literature with *In paren-thesis*, a retrospective interpretation of his experiences in the First World War. (Colour Plate 4)

KARIN JONZEN. Born 1914. Slade School of Art; the Academy, Stockholm. Member of the London Group. (Plate 3)

PETER LANYON. Born at St Ives, Cornwall, 1918. Educated at Penzance and Clifton College, Bristol. Served in the Royal Air Force, 1940–6, in the Middle East and Italy. Founder Member of St Ives Crypt Group and the Penwith Society of Arts. (Plate 35)

EDWARD LE BAS. Born in 1904, of Channel Islands descent. Cambridge University Architectural School and the Royal College of Art. Member of the London Group (1942) and an Associate of the Royal Academy (1943). (Plate 40)

LOUIS LE BROCQUY. Born in Ireland, 1917. Without academic training, he exhibited first in London in 1945. (Plate 49)

WYNDHAM LEWIS. Born 1884. Studied at the Slade School. Founded the Vorticist Movement (1914); founded and edited the magazine *Blast* (1914), *The Tyro* (1921) and *The Enemy* (1927). Original member of the London Group (1914). Author of many works of satire, fiction and criticism. For further details see his autobiography, *Rude Assignment* (1950). (Plate 38)

L. S. LOWRY. Born in Manchester, 1887. Manchester School of Art. He has exhibited at the Salon d'Automne, Paris, at the Royal Academy, London, and with the London Group. (Plate 16)

ROBERT MACBRYDE. Born in Ayrshire, Scotland, 1913. Worked for five years in factory and engineering works before entering Glasgow School of Art at 19. Studied in France and Italy, 1937–9. (Colour Plate 5)

F. E. MCWILLIAM. Born at Banbridge, Ireland, 1909. Slade School of Art, Paris. R.A.F. 1940–5 (service in the Far East). Teaches at the Slade School. (Plate 44)

BATESON MASON. Born near Bradford, 1910. Bradford College of Art; Royal College of Art. (Plate 21)

BERNARD MEADOWS. Born at Norwich, 1915. Norwich School of Art, 1934–6; Royal College of Art, 1938–40, 1946–8. Since 1936 has worked in the studio of Henry Moore. Teaches sculpture at the Chelsea School of Art. (Plate 57)

43

ROBERT MEDLEY. Born 1906. Studied at the Slade School of Art and in Paris. Member of the London Group and the London Artists' Association. (Plate 28)

JOHN MINTON. Born near Cambridge, 1917. St John's Wood School of Art, London. In 1938 went to Paris to study painting, and visited Belgium, Holland, Switzerland, and Provence, returning to England at the outbreak of war. Collaborated with Michael Ayrton on the décor for John Gielgud's production of *Macbeth* in 1942. (Plate 22)

HENRY MOORE. Born at Castleford, Yorkshire, 1898. Leeds School of Art, 1919. Royal College of Art. Travelling scholarship, 1925, France and Italy. Official War Artist, 1940–2. Trustee of the Tate Gallery, 1941–8. Member of the Royal Fine Art Commission. Hon. D.Lit., University of Leeds. Hon. Associate of the R.I.B.A. Awarded the International Sculpture Prize, Venice Biennale, 1948. (Plate 55)

RODRIGO MOYNIHAN, A.R.A. Born 1910. Studied at the Slade School of Art. Member of the London Group. (Plate 6)

JOHN NASH. Born in London, 1893. During the First World War he served with the Artists' Rifles and was commissioned to paint war pictures for the Imperial War Museum. He became a member of the London Group, the New English Art Club, and of the Society of Wood Engravers, and taught Design at the Royal College of Art. In the Second World War he was an official war artist. (Plate 14)

BEN NICHOLSON. Born at Denham, Bucks, in 1894. The son of the late Sir William Nicholson. Studied at the Slade School, in France and the U.S.A. (Colour Plate 1)

WINIFRED NICHOLSON. Born 1893. Taught painting in childhood by her grandfather, who was one of the pre-Raphaelite painters. Byam Shaw School and Paris. Travelled to India and Burma. (Plate 25)

EDUARDO PAOLOZZI. Born in Edinburgh, 1924. Edinburgh College of Art and Slade School of Art. Teacher at the Central School of Arts and Crafts, London. (Plate 62)

VICTOR PASMORE. Born at Chelsham, Surrey, 1908. No academic training, painting in spare time while in local government service, 1928–38. One of the founders of the Euston Road School in 1937, and one of its leading teachers. Member of the

London Group. Since 1948 he has painted in the abstract style. (Plate 58)

JOHN PIPER. Born at Epsom, Surrey, 1903. Richmond School of Art, and the Royal College of Art. Official war artist, Second World War. Has designed scenery and costumes for opera, ballet, and dramatic productions, and has written and illustrated books on architecture and topography. (Plate 26)

VIVIAN PITCHFORTH. Born at Wakefield, Yorkshire, 1895. Wakefield School of Art and Leeds School of Art, the Royal College of Art, London. Member of the London Group. Official war artist, Second World War. (Plate 17)

MARY POTTER. Born 1900. Beckenham Art School. Slade School of Art. Member of the London Group. (Plate 24)

CERI RICHARDS. Born at Swansea, Glamorganshire, 1903. Swansea School of Art and the Royal College of Art. Member of the London Group. (Plate 11)

WILLIAM ROBERTS. Born in London, 1895. St Martin's School of Art and the Slade School. During both the First and the Second World Wars he was an official artist. An original member of the Vorticist Group, and now a member of the London Group. (Plate 39)

CLAUDE ROGERS. Born in London, 1907. Slade School of Art. Member of the London Group. One of the founders of the Euston Road school, 1937. Teaches painting at the Slade School. (Plate 10)

MICHAEL ROTHENSTEIN. Born in 1908, younger son of Sir William Rothenstein. Chelsea School of Art and the Central School of Arts and Crafts, London. (Plate 50)

KENNETH ROWNTREE. Born at Scarborough, 1915. Ruskin School of Drawing, Oxford. Slade School of Art. Teacher at the Royal College of Art since 1948. (Plate 20)

WILLIAM SCOTT. Born 1913, of Irish and Scottish parents. Studied at the Royal Academy Schools. Served in Army in 1939–45 war. Teaches painting at the Bath Art School. (Colour Plate 2)

MATTHEW SMITH. Born at Halifax, 1879. The Manchester School of Art, the Slade School, London. In 1910 went on to Paris, where for a short time he came into contact with Matisse. (Plate 7)

RUSKIN SPEAR, A.R.A. Born 1911. Studied at Hammersmith School of Art and the Royal College of Art. Member of the London Group. (Plate 9)

STANLEY SPENCER, R.A. Born at Cookham, Berkshire, 1891. The Slade School, London. His service in Macedonia in the First World War provided him with the subjects for a set of mural paintings in the oratory of All Souls, Burghclere, Berkshire, 1926–33. Member of New English Art Club, 1919–27. Official war artist in the Second World War. (Plate 42)

GRAHAM SUTHERLAND. Born in London, 1903. Goldsmiths' College School of Art, University of London. Here he specialized in engraving, which occupied the greater part of his time until 1930. Visiting teacher at Chelsea School of Art, 1927–40. Commissioned to paint a *Crucifixion* for St Matthew's, Northampton, 1946. Has also designed for ceramics, tapestry, and textiles. An official artist during the Second World War. (Colour Plate 6)

GEOFFREY TIBBLE. Born 1909. Reading School of Art, 1925, Slade School of Art. During the 1930's worked in an abstract style, but later began to paint in the style which now characterizes his work. Member of the London Group. (Plate 41)

WILLIAM TOWNSEND. Born in London, 1909. Slade School of Art. Travelled in Egypt, Italy and North Africa. Army School of Education, 1945–6. Now teaches at the Slade School. Part-time teacher, Camberwell School of Art, 1946–9. (Plate 18)

JOHN TUNNARD. Born at Sandy, Bedfordshire, 1900. Studied at Royal College of Art. Began career as textile designer but later devoted himself to painting. Member of the London Group. (Plate 34)

WILLIAM TURNBULL. Born 1922. Slade School of Art. (Plate 61)

KEITH VAUGHAN. Born at Selsey Bill, Sussex, 1912. A designer in an advertising agency until the outbreak of the Second World War. (Plate 47)

JOHN WELLS. Born in London, 1907. University College and Hospital, London. Medical practice, Isles of Scilly, 1936–45. Practised painting at Newlyn since 1945. (Plate 29)

BRYAN WYNTER. Born 1916. Studied at the Slade School of Art. (Plate 33)

A LIST OF BOOKS

GENERAL

MARRIOTT, CHARLES: *Modern Movements in Painting*, London (Chapman & Hall), 1920

WILENSKI, R. H.: *The Modern Movement in Art*, London (Faber & Gwyer), 1927

READ, HERBERT: *Art Now*, London (Faber & Faber), 1st edn, 1933. Revised and enlarged edn, 1948

READ, HERBERT (Ed.): *Surrealism*, London (Faber & Faber), 1936

IRONSIDE, ROBIN: *Painting since 1939*, London (Longmans, Green & Co for the British Council), 1947

BERTRAM, ANTHONY: A Century of British Painting. London (The Studio, Ltd), 1951

MANIFESTOS

UNIT ONE: *The Modern Movement in English Architecture, Painting and Sculpture*. Edited by Herbert Read. London (Cassell), 1934

CIRCLE: *International Survey of Constructive Art*. Editors: J. L. Martin, Ben Nicholson, N. Gabo. London (Faber & Faber), 1937

THE PAINTER'S OBJECT: Edited by Myfanwy Evans. London (Gerald Howe), 1937

MONOGRAPHS

THE PENGUIN MODERN PAINTERS: Edited by Sir Kenneth Clark.

Henry Moore. By Geoffrey Grigson. 1944

Graham Sutherland. By Edward Sackville-West. 1944

Duncan Grant. By Raymond Mortimer. 1944

Paul Nash. By Herbert Read. 1944

Matthew Smith. By Philip Hendy. 1944

John Piper. By John Betjeman. 1944

Edward Burra. By John Rothenstein. 1945

Victor Pasmore. By Clive Bell. 1945

Edward Bawden. By J. M. Richards. 1947

Stanley Spencer. By Eric Newton. 1947

Frances Hodgkins. By Myfanwy Evans. 1948

William Nicholson. By Robert Nichols. 1948

Ben Nicholson. By John Summerson. 1948

David Jones. By Robin Ironside. 1949

AUGUSTUS JOHN. By John Rothenstein. (Phaidon Press), 1944

STANLEY SPENCER. By Elizabeth Rothenstein. (Phaidon Press), 1945

HENRY MOORE: *Sculpture and Drawings*. With an Introduction by Herbert Read. London (Lund Humphries & Co), 1944. Revised and enlarged edition, 1949

PAUL NASH: *Paintings, Drawings and Illustrations*. Edited by Margot Eates with essays by Herbert Read, John Rothenstein, E. H. Ramsden and Philip James. London (Lund Humphries), 1948

BEN NICHOLSON: *Paintings, Reliefs, Drawings*. With an Introduction by Herbert Read. London (Lund Humphries), 1948

GRAHAM SUTHERLAND: Edited by Robert Melville, London (The Ambassador Editions), 1950.

BARBARA HEPWORTH: *Sculptress*. With an Introduction by William Gibson. London (Faber & Faber for the Shenval Press), 1946

1. AUGUSTUS JOHN, O.M.: Portrait of Matthew Smith. 1947–8

2. JACOB EPSTEIN: Vaughan Williams, O.M. 1950

3. KARIN JONZEN: Bust. 1949

4. LAWRENCE GOWING: Miss Baker. 1948

5. WILLIAM COLDSTREAM: Portrait of Mrs. G. A. Auden. 1937

6. RODRIGO MOYNIHAN: Still-life with Figure. 1943

7. MATTHEW SMITH: Elizabeth Raynham. 1941

8. LUCIAN FREUD: Girl with Roses. 1947–8

9. RUSKIN SPEAR, A.R.A.: Barmaid. 1947

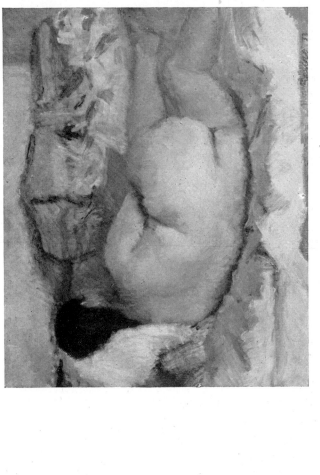

10. CLAUDE ROGERS: Nude. 1937

11. CERI RICHARDS: The Red Skirt. 1949

12. H. E. DU PLESSIS: Russell Square. 1945

13. EDWARD BAWDEN: A Dry Moat. 1948

14. JOHN NASH, A.R.A.: The River Brett, Higham. 1950

15. W. G. GILLIES: Gruinard. 1948

16. L. S. LOWRY: Industrial City. 1948

17. VIVIAN PITCHFORTH: Night Transport. 1940

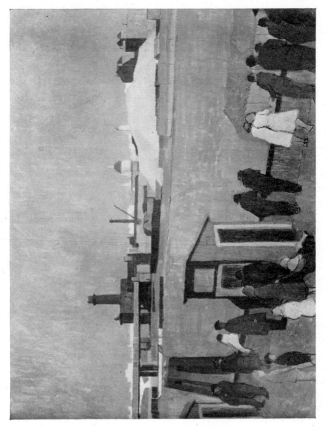

18. WILLIAM TOWNSEND: South Bank, 1948.

19. TRISTRAM HILLIER: Fishing Boats. 1946

20. KENNETH ROWNTREE: Lion Dining-Rooms. 1949

21. BATESON MASON: Fulham by Moonlight. 1949

22. JOHN MINTON · London Bridge, c. 1945

23. LEONARD APPLEBEE: Bethania. 1947

24. MARY POTTER: Jessamine. 1943

25. WINIFRED NICHOLSON: Honeysuckle and Sweet Peas – Contrast of Pinks. c. 1930

26. JOHN PIPER: Cheltenham: Composite of Houses in Priory
Parade. 1950

27. ALAN DAVIE: Music of the Autumn Landscape. 1948

28. ROBERT MEDLEY: A Summer Day. 1950

29. JOHN WELLS: Old Sea Port. 1949

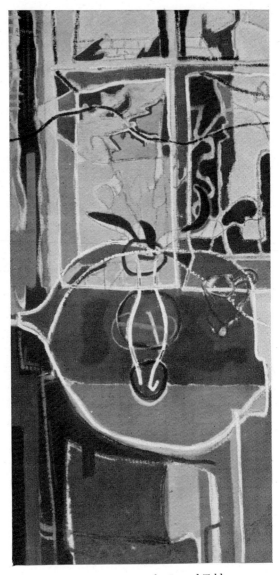

30. PATRICK HERON: The Round Table. 1950

31. PRUNELLA CLOUGH: Fishermen in a Boat. 1949

32. JOHN ARMSTRONG: Encounter. 1947

33. BRYAN WYNTER: Foreshore with Gulls. 1949

34. JOHN TUNNARD: Weather Forecast. 1945

35. PETER LANYON: Portreath. 1949

36. EDWARD BURRA: St Peter and the High Priest's Servant.
1950

37. ROY DE MAISTRE: The Deposition. 1946

38. WYNDHAM LEWIS: The Armada. 1937

39. WILLIAM ROBERTS: The Mothers. 1944

40. EDWARD LE BAS, A.R.A.: Barmaid at the Garrick. 1944

41. GEOFFREY TIBBLE: Pay Day. 1950

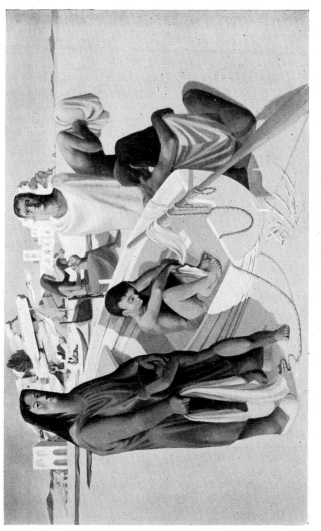

43. MICHAEL AYRTON: Afternoon in Ischia. 1947

44. F. E. McWILLIAM: Father and Daughter. 1949

45. FRANK DOBSON, A.R.A.: Study for Leisure. 1950

46. JOHN CRAXTON: Galatas. 1947

47. KEITH VAUGHAN: Oyster Fisherman, No. 1. 1947–8

48. ROBERT COLQUHOUN: Girl with a Circus Goat. 1948

49. LOUIS LE BROCQUY: Man Creating a Bird. 1948

50. MICHAEL ROTHENSTEIN: Cockerel and Plough. 1950

51. MERLYN EVANS: The Jail. 1950

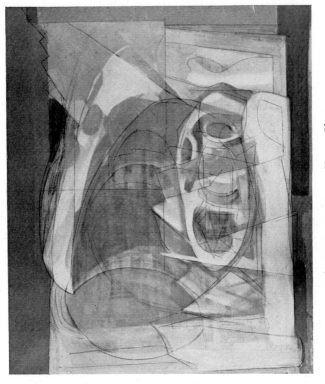

52. W. BARNS-GRAHAM: Upper Glacier. 1950

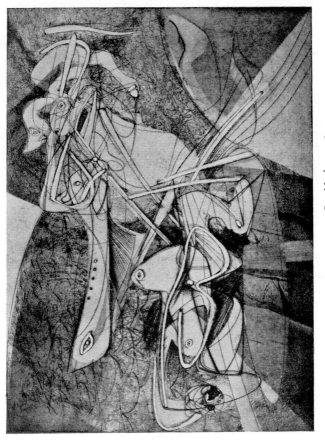

53. S. W. HAYTER: Sea Myth. 1946–7

54. WILLIAM GEAR: Black Tree. 1950

55. HENRY MOORE: Standing Figure (detail). 1950

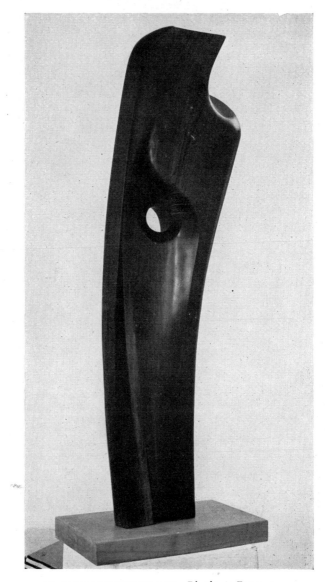

56. BARBARA HEPWORTH: Rhythmic Form. 1950

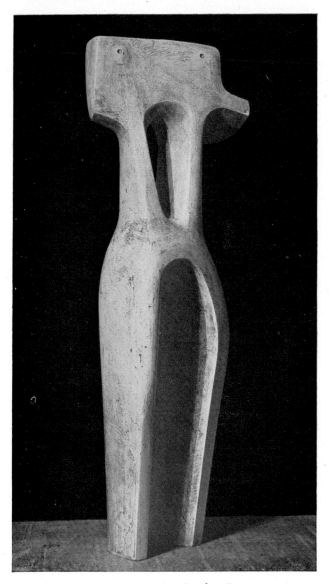

57. BERNARD MEADOWS: Standing Figure. 1950

58. VICTOR PASMORE: Rectangular Motif – Brown and White. 1949

59. ROBERT ADAMS: Figure. 1949

60. REG BUTLER: Head. 1948–9

61. WILLIAM TURNBULL: Metamorphoses. 1949

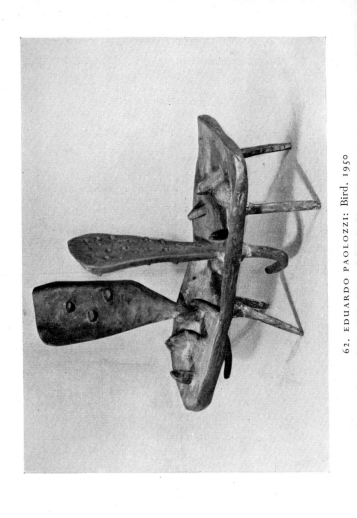

62. EDUARDO PAOLOZZI: Bird. 1950

63. LYNN CHADWICK: Mobile. 1950.

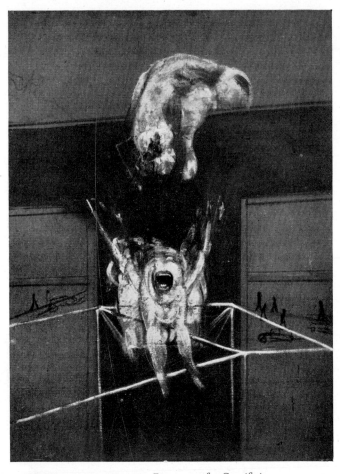

64. FRANCIS BACON: Fragment of a Crucifixion. 1950